Bizarre Beasts

And other oddities of nature

Text by Anita Ganeri

BIG FACE
BOOKS™

ISBN 1–55280–248–5
Library of Congress Catalog Card Number: 95–83534

Copyright © 1995 by Marshall Editions Developments Limited, London

All rights reserved. No part of the contents of this book may be reproduced without the written permission of the publisher.

Originated by Master Image, Singapore.
Printed and bound in China

This Edition Exclusive to [BIG FACE BOOKS]

printed in china

ACKNOWLEDGEMENTS

The publishers would like to thank the following artists for illustrating this book:

Elizabeth Kay for pages 12–13, 18–19, 28–29; **Eric Robson** (Garden Studio) for pages 8–9, 16–17, 22–23, 24–25, 26–27; **Bernard Robinson** for this page and pages 20–21; **Simon Turvey** (Wildlife Art Agency) for pages 6–7, 10–11, 14–15.

Editor: **Charlotte Evans**
Designer: **Ralph Pitchford**
Managing Editor: **Kate Phelps**
Art Director: **Branka Surla**
Editorial Director: **Cynthia O'Brien**
Research: **Lynda Wargen**
Production: **Janice Storr**

▲ The bizarre-looking giant anteater sniffs out ants' nests with its long, pointed snout. It then tears open the nest with its claws and picks up the ants with its long, sticky tongue.

Contents

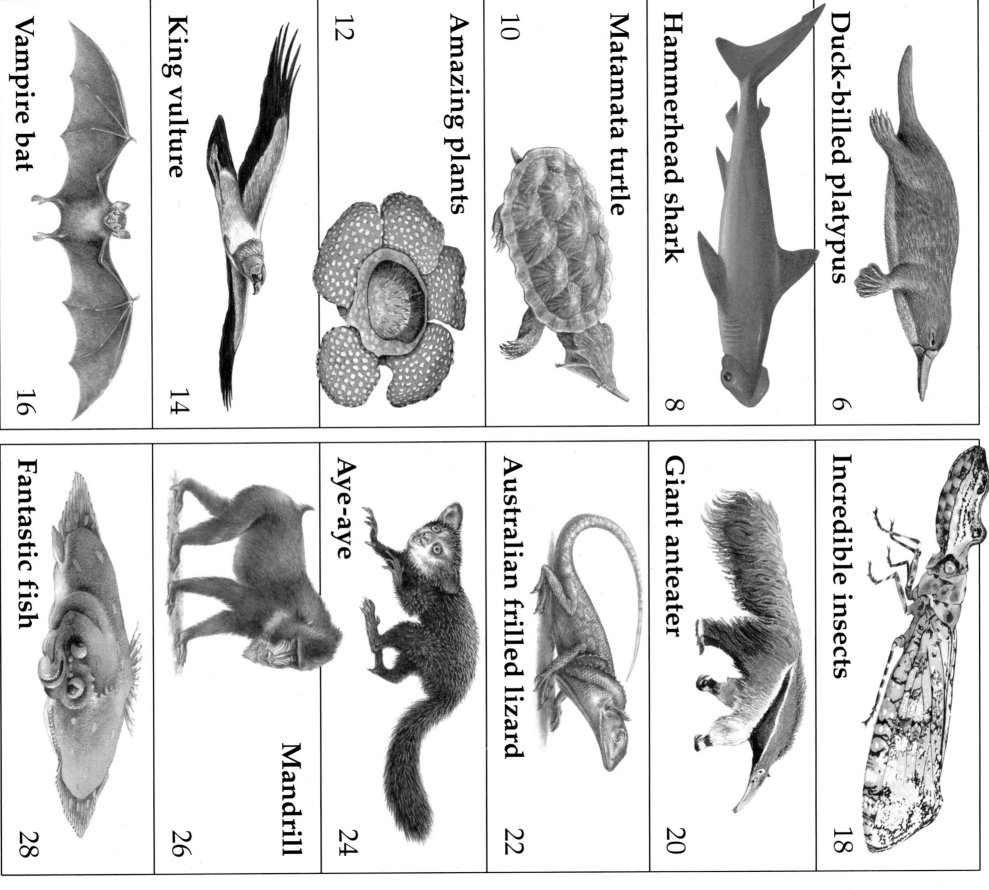

Duck-billed platypus

When the first platypus skin arrived in Britain from Australia in 1799, scientists dismissed it as a fake. It seemed to come from an animal with a furry body like a beaver's, a beak like a duck's, and it had webbed feet. Surely such a bizarre beast could not really exist? People thought the skin must have been made of bits and pieces sewn together. But the skin was not fake. It belonged to a very unusual type of mammal — the duck-billed platypus.

Most mammals give birth to live young which feed on their mother's milk. The platypus is one of a very few mammals to lay eggs. The only other egg-laying mammals, or monotremes, are the two types of spiny anteaters, or echidnas, which are also found in Australia.

▼ Male platypuses have sharp spurs on the heels of their back feet which they use for jabbing enemies or rival males. The spurs can inject enough venom to kill an animal as big as a dog. The poison is not fatal to people, but it can cause agonizing pain.

▲ The platypus's front feet are webbed for fast swimming. They also have strong, sharp claws for digging out the burrows where they live. On land, the platypus curls up the skin of its webbed feet so it can move around.

DUCK-BILLED PLATYPUS

Bearing young
The female lays two or three eggs in a grass-lined burrow. The newborn babies are blind and hairless. They suckle on their mother's milk for three to four months.

Length: up to 2 feet
Weight: up to 5 pounds

Platypus eggs are white, about the size of marbles, and have soft, sticky shells. They hatch after about 10 days.

Where do they live?
Beside slow-moving, freshwater streams, rivers, and lakes in eastern Australia and Tasmania.

▶ The platypus hunts for food under the water. It uses its soft, leathery bill for scooping insect larvae, shellfish, frogs, and worms from the riverbed. The platypus stores its catch in its cheeks until they are full; then it surfaces to chew and swallow its food.

▶ While it searches for its food, the platypus closes its eyes, ears, and nostrils to keep out water. For locating prey, it relies instead on its highly sensitive bill.

▶ The platypus's whole body is adapted for life on the river bank. Its thick fur is warm and waterproof. Its body is streamlined for swimming and strong and flexible for burrowing.

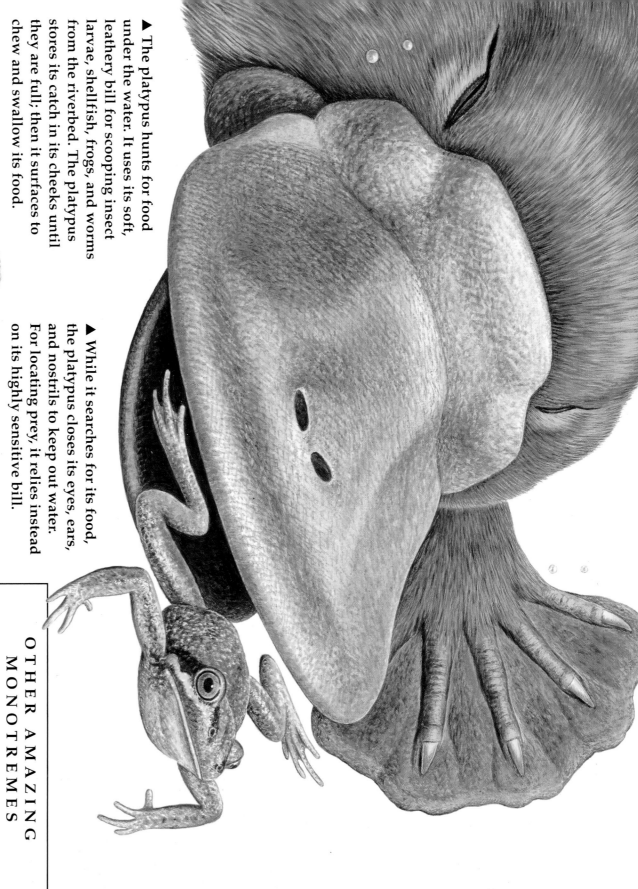

OTHER AMAZING MONOTREMES

Short-beaked echidna
This echidna uses its spines for protection, curling up into a spiky ball if danger threatens. The spines are sharp enough to pierce leather.

Long-beaked echidna
This echidna uses its long, thin snout to sniff out earthworms which it then hooks onto its long, sticky tongue.

Hammerhead shark

It has a shark's body, a shark's tail, and a shark's razor-sharp teeth. It also has one of the strangest heads of any creature, in the sea or on land. As its name suggests, the hammerhead shark has a hammer-shaped head, with its eyes located at each end of the "T" and its nostrils slightly farther in. Its bizarre appearance may help it detect prey or swim faster—no one is absolutely sure. Each of the eight species of hammerhead has a slightly different shaped hammer, which is useful for identification. Hammerhead sharks live mainly in warm, tropical oceans, migrating in summer to cooler waters and returning as winter sets in. By day, the sharks swim in large schools, up to 100 strong. By night, the schools split up, and the sharks set off alone to hunt for their prey.

▶ Hammerhead sharks feed mainly on fish and invertebrates. They are especially fond of stingrays, which lie buried on the sandy seafloor. Hammerheads seem to be unharmed by the stingrays' poisonous spines—one shark found had more than 50 stingray spines still stuck in its mouth.

▶ Sharks detect their food by sight and smell, and by picking up tiny electrical charges coming from their prey. The shape of a hammerhead's head means that its sense organs are more widely spaced than normal, which may help it locate prey more quickly and accurately. Its head may also act as a natural hydrofoil, to stop the shark from pitching and rolling as it swims.

OTHER AMAZING SHARKS

Goblin shark
This bizarre-looking shark has a flabby, pink body and an extra-long, pointed snout. No one knows what the snout is used for.

Carpet shark
The carpet shark is named after its pattern of spots and stripes, which helps it hide on the seafloor. The flaps of skin around its mouth are also used for camouflage, breaking up the shark's outline and making it harder to see.

Frilled shark
With its long, narrow body, the frilled shark looks more like an eel than a shark. It gets its name from the frilled edges of its gills.

Sawshark
Sawsharks kill their prey by slashing around in a school of small fish with their bladelike "saws." Baby sawsharks are born with their saw teeth folded back to avoid injuring their mother.

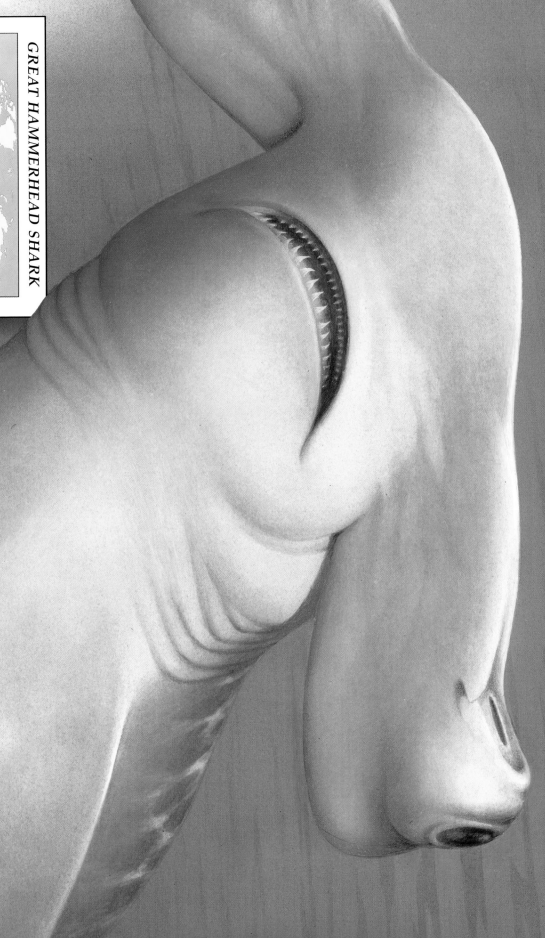

Where do they live?
In temperate and tropical oceans around the world. Uncommon in colder water, below 70° F.

Length: up to 20 feet
Weight: up to 2,000 pounds

Bearing young
Females give birth in spring or early summer. A litter may contain up to 40 baby sharks, which are known as pups.

▲ Many sharks lay soft-shelled eggs but hammerheads give birth to live young that look like miniature versions of their parents. Young hammerheads are born headfirst, with the tip of their hammerhead folded backward to make them more streamlined for birth.

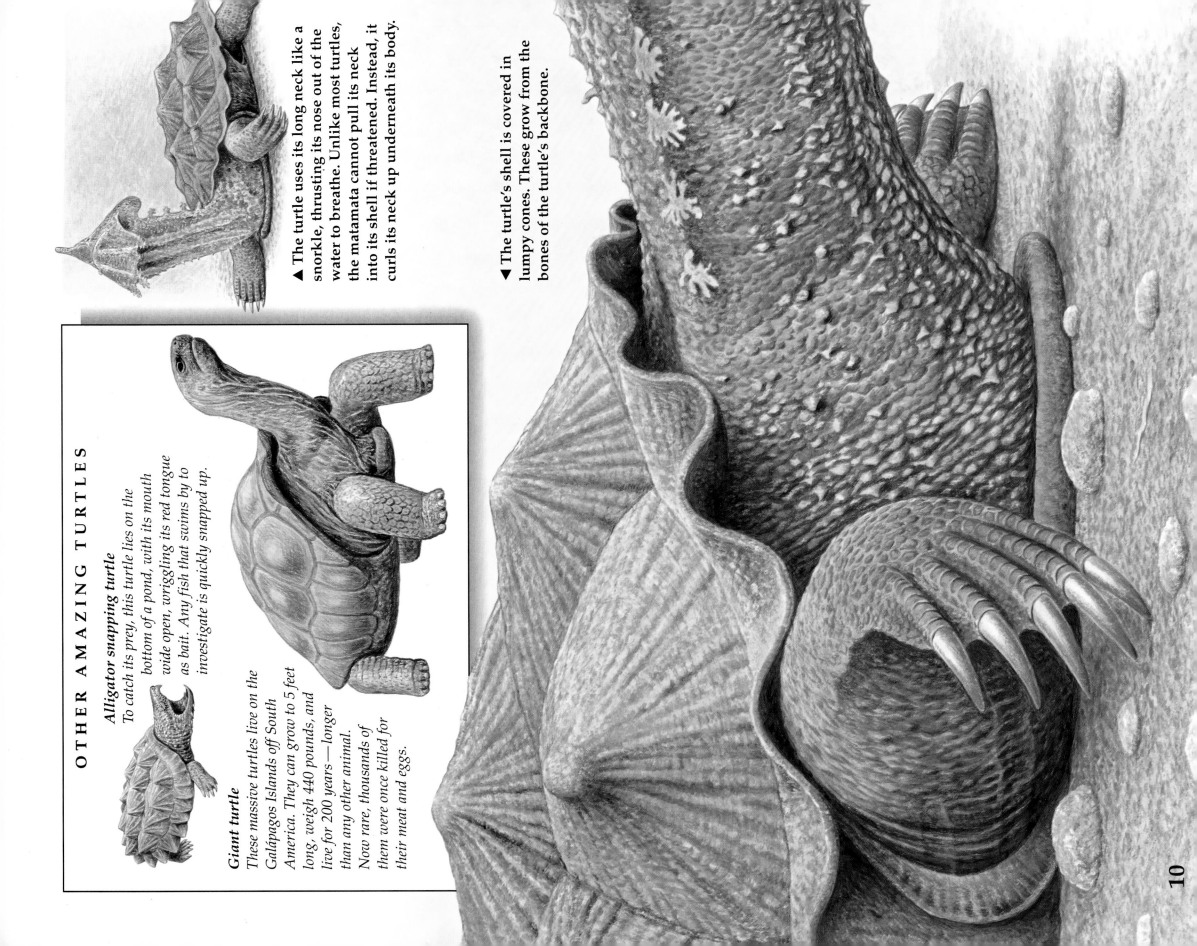

▲ The turtle uses its long neck like a snorkle, thrusting its nose out of the water to breathe. Unlike most turtles, the matamata cannot pull its neck into its shell if threatened. Instead, it curls its neck up underneath its body.

▼ The turtle's shell is covered in lumpy cones. These grow from the bones of the turtle's backbone.

OTHER AMAZING TURTLES

Alligator snapping turtle
To catch its prey, this turtle lies on the bottom of a pond, with its mouth wide open, wriggling its red tongue as bait. Any fish that swims by to investigate is quickly snapped up.

Giant turtle
These massive turtles live on the Galápagos Islands off South America. They can grow to 5 feet long, weigh 440 pounds, and live for 200 years — longer than any other animal. Now rare, thousands of them were once killed for their meat and eggs.

Matamata turtle

One of the oddest looking of all turtles, the matamata turtle lives in swamps and slow-moving rivers in South America. Its bizarre appearance serves a very useful purpose when it comes to catching food. Camouflaged by its strange body shape, the turtle lies on the riverbed, with its mouth wide open, waiting to ambush passing fish. Its limbs and flattened head are ruffled with frills and shreds of skin and, as it waits, keeping perfectly still, it looks just like a pile of harmless weeds and garbage. Small fish who try to nibble at these skinny fronds should beware—they will be quickly swallowed up.

▼ The matamata has a huge mouth for gobbling up prey. When a fish swims by, the turtle shoots its head and mouth forward. As it does so, its throat and neck stretch, and the turtle sucks in water like a suction pump. Anything unlucky enough to be in the water is immediately swallowed.

▲ The skin on the turtle's neck is loose and wrinkled, and looks like a large ruffle. It is thought that this frill helps to attract fish and other prey, such as crustaceans, toward the turtle's mouth. The matamata's skin is a mottled, greenish-brown color, as is its shell, which is covered in algae. All these features help to camouflage the turtle as it lies on the riverbed.

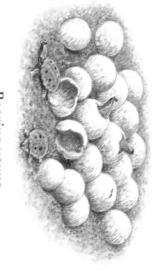

Amazing plants

Plants range in size from tiny water plants, no bigger than a speck of dust, to huge giant redwood trees hundreds of feet high. Like animals, they have a variety of special features, tricks, and disguises to keep themselves from being eaten, to make sure their flowers get pollinated, and to survive heat, cold, and drought.

▶ The very peculiar ant plant lives on the branches of mangrove trees. The plant's swollen stem is crisscrossed with tiny tunnels, home to hundreds of ants. In return for the shelter it offers, the plant gets nourishment from the ants' droppings and leftovers.

▶ Rafflesia flowers can measure 3 feet across—the biggest flowers of any plant. They are also the smelliest flowers, reeking of rotten meat. This is a trick designed to attract flies for pollination. The flies think they are in for a good meal!

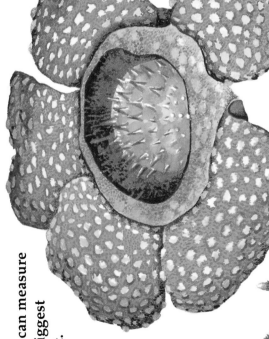

▶ Kangaroo paws rely on birds for pollination. Some grow very tall and are extra-strong to support a bird's weight. While a bird sips nectar from the tube-shaped flowers, its feathers are dusted with pollen. This is carried to the next flower it visits to pollinate it.

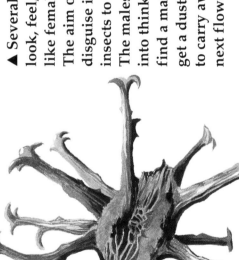

▶ Several types of orchids look, feel, and even smell like female wasps or bees. The aim of their amazing disguise is to attract male insects to their flowers. The males are tricked into thinking they will find a mate. In fact, they get a dusting of pollen to carry away to the next flower.

▶ For a seed to develop into a new plant, it must find a suitable place to grow. The extraordinary grapple plant hitches a ride on a passing elephant or rhinoceros. Its seed pod has sharp hooks that dig into the animal's foot as it walks by. Then the pod is carried until it breaks open, scattering its seeds.

12

PLANTS THAT EAT MEAT

Most green plants make their own food, but some eat meat. These plants trap insects with their odd-shaped leaves. Then they slowly digest the insects' bodies and absorb the nutrients.

▼ Pitcher plants have juglike traps at the ends of their leaves. Insects, attracted by the plant's bright color and sweet smell, land on the rim, fall down the slippery walls, and are digested in a pool of liquid at the bottom.

▼ The leaves of the Venus's-flytrap normally lie open. But, if an insect lands on one and brushes against the sensitive hairs on its surface, the leaf snaps shut, trapping the victim inside.

▼ The leaves of the sundew plant are covered in tiny hairs that have sticky droplets on the end. Insects get stuck to the leaves, which then fold over to digest them as they struggle to escape.

▼ A strangler fig grows from a seed dropped high on a tree branch by a bat or a bird. Slowly, its roots grow down to the ground, where they can begin to draw water and nutrients from the soil. The fig grows quickly, until its roots completely strangle the tree within it. Deprived of light and water, the tree often rots away and dies.

▼ For most of the year, this unusual desert plant is very difficult to spot among the gravel and stones where it grows. It has two fleshy leaves, which it uses for storing water. These match the color of the surrounding rock exactly. It gives itself away only when a large flower shoots up in the groove between the leaves.

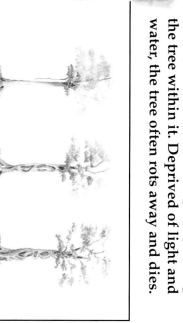

▼ The bizarre baobab tree has a swollen trunk, shaped like a giant bottle. When it rains, the tree sucks in water to store in its trunk for use in the dry season. Its trunk can swell up to 33 feet around its girth.

▼ In the rainforest, there is great competition to reach the sunlight. The pandanus palm has long, stilt-like roots that it uses to prop itself up. The long roots help the palm to grow taller than the trees surrounding it.

▼ These bloodlike blisters on the trunk of a rain forest tree are patches of lichen. Lichens are tough, slow-growing plants that are also very strange, because they are a partnership between an alga and a fungus.

King vulture

When an animal dies or is killed in the forest or on the open plains, vultures are quick to gather at the scene. They are nature's garbage collectors, stripping the animal's carcass of any scraps of meat and picking the bones clean. Vultures arrive in large groups, squabbling among themselves to get a share of the feast.

The king vulture is so named because it usually beats off its smaller rivals. The king vulture's fearsome appearance is directly linked to its feeding habits. It has sharp eyes for spotting a kill, a powerful, hooked bill for cutting and tearing meat, and, strangest of all, a bare, brightly colored head.

▲ King vultures circle and soar above the trees on rising currents of warm air, called thermals. They tend to follow the movements of other vultures to find their prey. Once the vultures spot a carcass, they swoop down, with the king vultures close behind.

▲ With its striking black and white feathers and vivid head, the king vulture is a distinctive bird. Young king vultures are born almost completely black. They do not grow their adult plumage until they are three to four years old.

KING VULTURE

Where do they live?
In the rainforests and savannas of Central and South America, from Mexico to Argentina, and in Trinidad.

Wing span: up to 6½ feet
Weight: up to 8 pounds

Bearing young
The female lays a single egg in a tree stump. After about two months it hatches and both parents take care of the chick for up to two years.

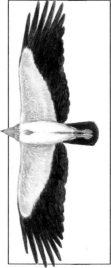

Spoonbill
Spoonbills feed in the water, sweeping their spoon-shaped bills gracefully from side to side, sifting out small fish, shellfish, and insects.

Brown pelican
Pelicans have beaks like huge fishing nets, with stretchy pouches of skin for scooping fish out of the water.

Marabou stork
These grotesque-looking birds are scavengers. They feed on carrion, garbage dumps, and on animals fleeing a grass fire. In India, they can be seen near funeral pyres.

Cassowary
This bird uses its hard, bony head as a helmet to crash through the jungle. Its colorful wattles may be used for signaling.

▲ The king vulture uses its strong, sharp, hooked bill to tear flesh. It is a scavenger, feeding on carrion (dead and rotting meat) killed by other animals. The vulture's head and neck are bare of feathers. This prevents them from getting clogged with blood as the vulture feeds. Vultures also wipe their head and neck on the ground after feeding to clean them.

▲ The strange, brightly colored folds and flaps of skin around the vulture's bill are called wattles. They are thought to help the vulture attract a mate for breeding. Each vulture's colors and markings are slightly different and act as a guide to the bird's age, identity, health, and strength.

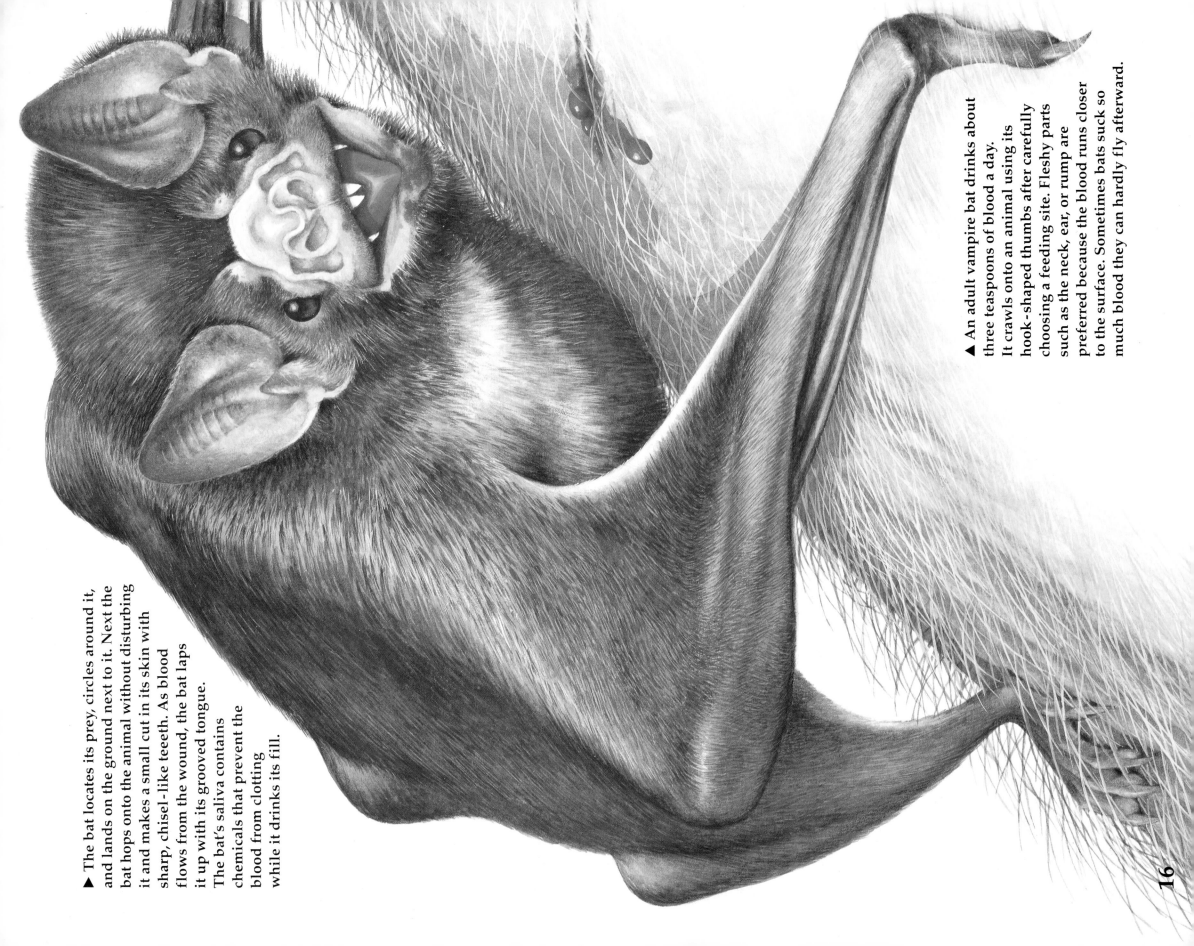

▲ The bat locates its prey, circles around it, and lands on the ground next to it. Next the bat hops onto the animal without disturbing it and makes a small cut in its skin with sharp, chisel-like teeeth. As blood flows from the wound, the bat laps it up with its grooved tongue. The bat's saliva contains chemicals that prevent the blood from clotting while it drinks its fill.

▲ An adult vampire bat drinks about three teaspoons of blood a day. It crawls onto an animal using its hook-shaped thumbs after carefully choosing a feeding site. Fleshy parts such as the neck, ear, or rump are preferred because the blood runs closer to the surface. Sometimes bats suck so much blood they can hardly fly afterward.

16

Vampire bat

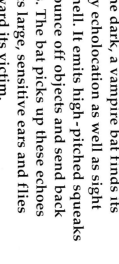

▲In the dark, a vampire bat finds its prey by echolocation as well as sight and smell. It emits high-pitched squeaks that bounce off objects and send back echoes. The bat picks up these echoes with its large, sensitive ears and flies off toward its victim.

You've probably heard the chilling tale of Count Dracula, the famous vampire who leaves his castle by night to suck the blood of his sleeping victims. But did you know that the legend may be based on a tiny, quite ordinary-looking bat that lives in South and Central America? The vampire bat lives on the blood of cattle, pigs, and horses, although occasionally it has been known to attack humans. A vampire bat has teeth as sharp as a razor, but the victim rarely feels a bat's bite. Farmers treat vampire bats as pests because their blood-thirsty habits can spread deadly diseases, such as rabies, among their animals.

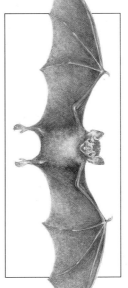

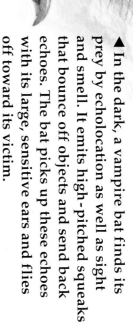

Where do they live?
Central and South America, from northern Mexico south to Chile, Uruguay, and Argentina.

Wing span: up to 8 inches
Weight: up to 1½ ounces

Bearing young
A female gives birth to one baby that she carries with her for its first few days. The baby is left in the roost while the mother hunts for food. It can fly after about three weeks.

▲By day, large groups of vampire bats hang upside down in caves or hollow trees, holding on tight with their hooked claws. When darkness falls, they leave their roost to hunt for food.

OTHER AMAZING BATS

Australian ghost bat
This bat has pale, ghostly wings. The strange skin flaps on its face help it to direct squeaks of sound as it hunts.

Hammerhead bat
The shape and size of the male hammerhead bat's bizarre-looking head help it to amplify its loud mating call.

Horseshoe bat
The horseshoe-shaped flaps of skin around this bat's nose are also used to direct sound for hunting at night.

Incredible insects

There are more than a million known species of insects in the world, with many millions more still waiting to be discovered. They come in an amazing variety of colors, shapes, patterns, and designs, and have a wide range of special features. These markings and features are not simply for show: they have a practical purpose. Some help to hide insects from their enemies, and some are used as weapons. Other features help insects find food or homes. For an insect, looking as bizarre as possible may be a matter of life or death.

▶ Mole crickets, like real moles, have shovel-like front legs for digging through soil. As they burrow, they munch through underground roots with their special scissorlike mouthparts.

MASTERS OF DISGUISE

Many insects are disguised to look like something else to avoid detection by their enemies or by their prey. Often their shapes and colors closely resemble the plants they live on.

▼ Thorn bugs are superbly camouflaged insects. They cling to a twig and hold their bodies completely still so that they look exactly like the sharp thorns of a plant and are of no interest to a hungry bird.

▲ The South American grasshopper fools its enemies into mistaking it for an inedible stick. It even sways slightly, as if being blown by the breeze. Many insects mimic sticks, twigs, and leaves.

▼ The flower mantis looks just like the tropical flowers it rests on, with its wings and body resembling the pink and white petals. Any insect coming too close to the mantis is snapped up and eaten alive.

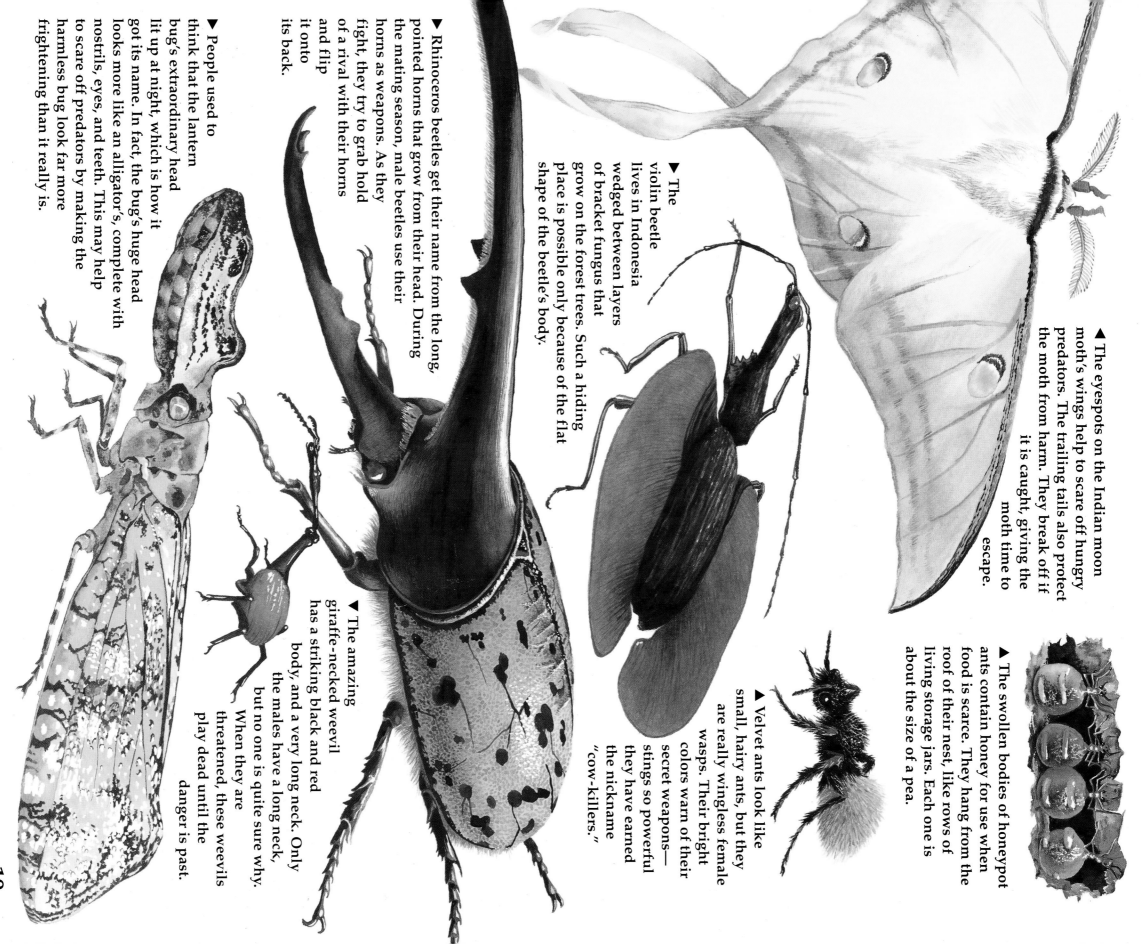

▶ People used to think that the lantern bug's extraordinary head lit up at night, which is how it got its name. In fact, the bug's huge head looks more like an alligator's, complete with nostrils, eyes, and teeth. This may help to scare off predators by making the harmless bug look far more frightening than it really is.

▶ Rhinoceros beetles get their name from the long, pointed horns that grow from their head. During the mating season, male beetles use their horns as weapons. As they fight, they try to grab hold of a rival with their horns and flip it onto its back.

▶ The amazing giraffe-necked weevil has a striking black and red body, and a very long neck, but no one is quite sure why. Only the males have a long neck. When they are threatened, these weevils play dead until the danger is past.

▶ The violin beetle lives in Indonesia wedged between layers of bracket fungus that grow on the forest trees. Such a hiding place is possible only because of the flat shape of the beetle's body.

▲ The eyespots on the Indian moon moth's wings help to scare off hungry predators. The trailing tails also protect the moth from harm. They break off if it is caught, giving the moth time to escape.

▶ The swollen bodies of honeypot ants contain honey for use when food is scarce. They hang from the roof of their nest, like rows of living storage jars. Each one is about the size of a pea.

▶ Velvet ants look like small, hairy ants, but they are really wingless female wasps. Their bright colors warn of their secret weapons—stings so powerful they have earned the nickname "cow-killers."

Giant anteater

Anteaters are strange and striking creatures that live on a diet of ants and termites. The giant anteater is the largest of the family, with a massive, bushy tail and an extremely long, pointed snout. The other, smaller anteaters are tree dwellers with smaller snouts. One type, the tamandua, is famous for the strong, unpleasant smell it releases, possibly for communication. This has earned it the nickname "stinker of the forest."

Anteaters spend much of their time asleep. The rest of the time they look for ants, their favorite food. The giant anteater sniffs out an ants' nest with its sensitive nose and rips the nest open with its sharp front claws. It does not have teeth, but uses its long, sticky tongue to pick up its prey. It can flick its tongue in and out at a staggering rate of 150 times a minute.

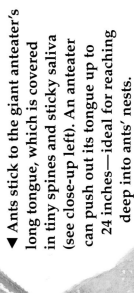

▼ Ants stick to the giant anteater's long tongue, which is covered in tiny spines and sticky saliva (see close-up left). An anteater can push out its tongue up to 24 inches—ideal for reaching deep into ants' nests.

GIANT ANTEATER

Where do they live?
In the forests and grasslands of Central and South America, east of the Andes Mountains.

Length: up to 6½ feet (head to tail)
Weight: up to 85 pounds

Bearing young
Giant anteaters usually meet only to breed. The mother gives birth to one baby that she carries on her back most of the time for up to a year.

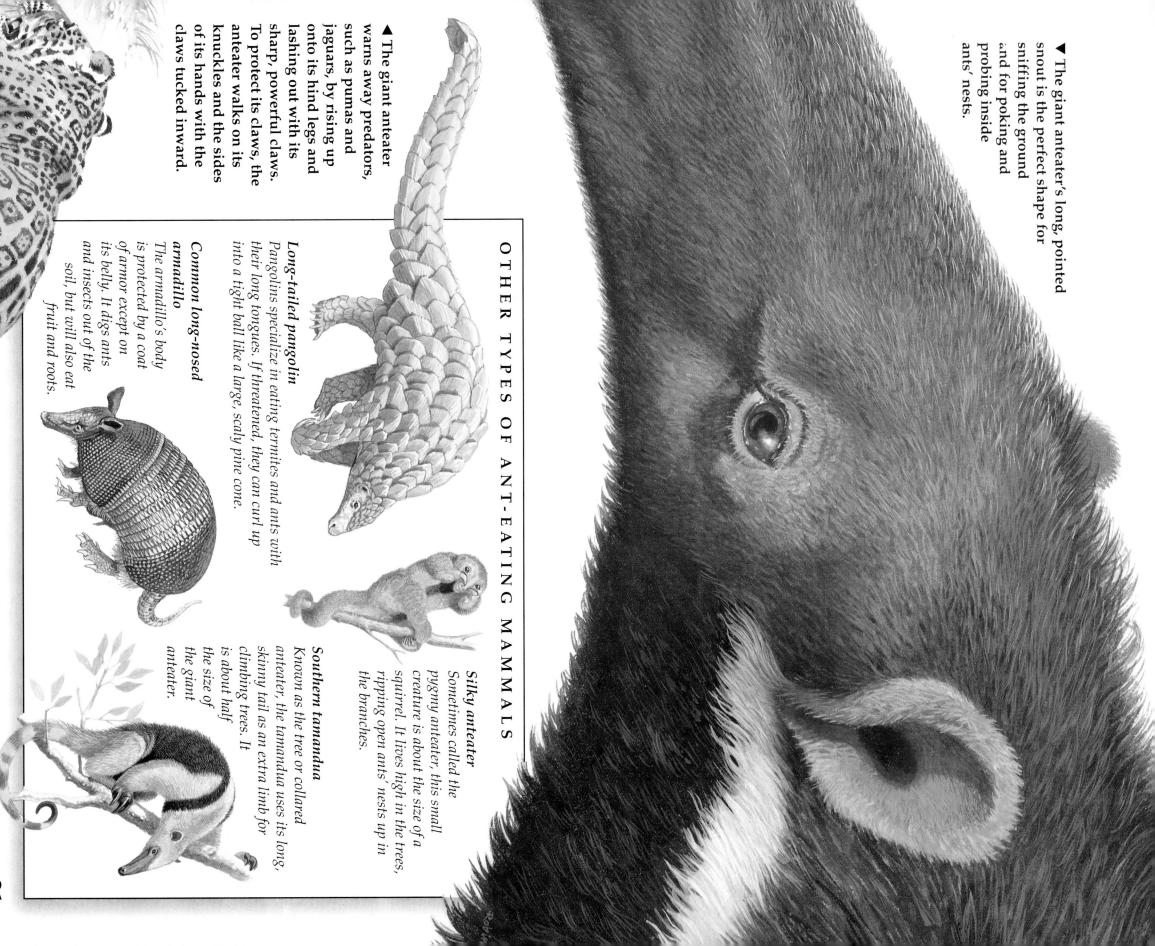

▲ The giant anteater's long, pointed snout is the perfect shape for sniffing the ground and for poking and probing inside ants' nests.

▲ The giant anteater warns away predators, such as pumas and jaguars, by rising up onto its hind legs and lashing out with its sharp, powerful claws. To protect its claws, the anteater walks on its knuckles and the sides of its hands with the claws tucked inward.

OTHER TYPES OF ANT-EATING MAMMALS

Long-tailed pangolin
Pangolins specialize in eating termites and ants with their long tongues. If threatened, they can curl up into a tight ball like a large, scaly pine cone.

Common long-nosed armadillo
The armadillo's body is protected by a coat of armor except on its belly. It digs ants and insects out of the soil, but will also eat fruit and roots.

Silky anteater
Sometimes called the pygmy anteater, this small creature is about the size of a squirrel. It lives high in the trees, ripping open ants' nests up in the branches.

Southern tamandua
Known as the tree or collared anteater, the tamandua uses its long, skinny tail as an extra limb for climbing trees. It is about half the size of the giant anteater.

Australian frilled lizard

The Australian frilled lizard startles attackers with an amazing display. When danger threatens, it opens its mouth wide, sways from side to side, and unfurls the magnificent ruffle of skin around its neck—which is raised by a series of gristly rods like the spokes of an umbrella. If this ploy does not work, it hisses loudly. The aim of the display is to make the lizard look much bigger and fiercer than it actually is, and most of the time it works perfectly. Its enemies, which include snakes, hawks, dingoes, and larger lizards, quickly flee from such a fearsome sight.

▲ The Australian frilled lizard usually keeps its amazing ruff folded flat against its body.
Active by day, the lizard lives among the branches of trees where it basks in the sun or hunts for prey. The color and texture of its skin help to camouflage the lizard against the bark of the tree.

AUSTRALIAN FRILLED LIZARD

Where do they live?
In forest trees across northern Australia and on the nearby islands of Papua New Guinea.

Length: up to 3 feet
Weight: up to 17½ ounces

Bearing young
The female lays two to eight eggs in the spring. They hatch about three months later, complete with tiny frills.

OTHER AMAZING LIZARDS

Jackson's chameleon
This chameleon swivels its eyes in different directions to locate prey, then shoots out a sticky tongue to reel it in. A master of disguise, it can change color in seconds.

Cylindrical skink
This lizard has very short legs, so when it wants to move quickly, it tucks them up under its body and slithers along like a snake.

Flying dragon
The flying dragon glides through the trees on wings formed from flaps of skin stretched between its front and back legs.

Thorny devil
The thorny devil lives in the deserts of Australia. Though harmless, its body bristles with sharp spikes. They protect it from enemies as it moves slowly across the sand, searching for ants and termites to eat.

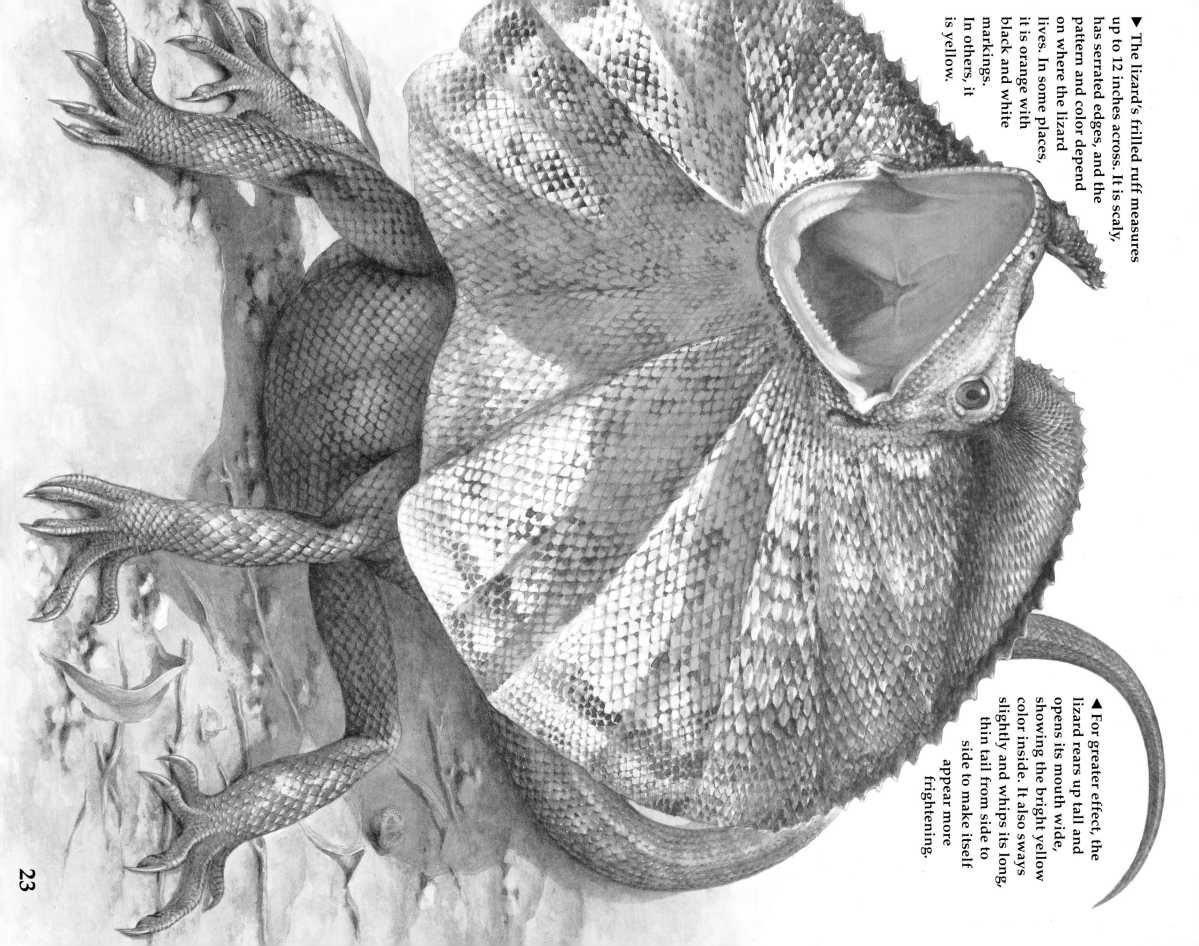

► The lizard's frilled ruff measures up to 12 inches across. It is scaly, has serrated edges, and the pattern and color depend on where the lizard lives. In some places, it is orange with black and white markings. In others, it is yellow.

▲ For greater effect, the lizard rears up tall and opens its mouth wide, showing the bright yellow color inside. It also sways slightly and whips its long, thin tail from side to side to make itself appear more frightening.

23

► The aye-aye has a thick, dark coat, flecked with silver, which makes it very difficult to see at night when it comes out to hunt. Its bushy tail is as long as its body.

► The aye-aye is a nocturnal animal, spending most of the day asleep in a treetop nest with its bushy tail curled around its body for warmth. It has a good sense of smell and an excellent sense of hearing, both of which are essential features for hunting prey at night. Aye-ayes spend most of their life alone, only coming together to breed.

24

Aye-aye

W ith large leathery ears like a bat's, a long bushy tail like a squirrel's, a foxlike face, and a cat-sized body, the aye-aye is one of the most unusual animals of all. This strange and secretive creature is a very rare type of lemur and is found only on the island of Madagascar in the Indian Ocean. Today, as few as 50 aye-ayes remain in the wild. Their survival is threatened not only by the loss of their rainforest habitat, but also by local superstition. Many local people believe that the aye-aye brings bad luck, and will kill any that they catch. Some zoos are now trying to breed aye-ayes in captivity so that they can be returned to the wild. The aye-aye's odd appearance is no accident. Each feature is an adaptation for a life spent among the rainforest trees.

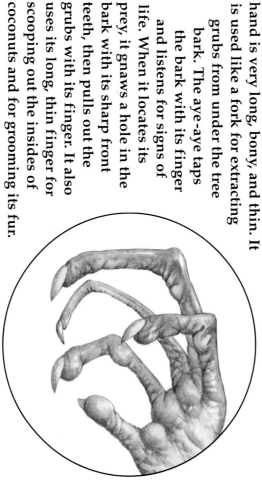

▶ The third finger on the aye-aye's hand is very long, bony, and thin. It is used like a fork for extracting grubs from under the tree bark. The aye-aye taps the bark with its finger and listens for signs of life. When it locates its prey, it gnaws a hole in the bark with its sharp front teeth, then pulls out the grubs with its finger. It also uses its long, thin finger for scooping out the insides of coconuts and for grooming its fur.

Where do they live?
In two areas of rainforest on the east coast of Madagascar and in a reserve on the nearby island of Nosy Mangabe.

Madagascar

Length: up to 32 inches (nose to tail)
Weight: up to 4½ pounds

Bearing young
The female gives birth to one baby every two to three years in a nest made of twigs and leaves high up in the fork of a tree. The mother carries the baby on her back while she searches for food.

OTHER BIZARRE NOCTURNAL ANIMALS

Western tarsier
The tarsier is a nocturnal animal with huge, round eyes for seeing in the dark and sharp hearing for finding prey. It leaps from tree to tree on its long back legs searching for insects.

Slender loris
The slender loris has large eyes for seeing at night, but it finds its food mainly by smell. Its small size and gray fur help it to hide from its enemies.

Lesser bush baby
The bush baby also hunts at night and sleeps by day. Its long, thick tail helps it keep its balance as it jumps through the tree tops.

25

▲ Male mandrills are the biggest monkeys of all — the females are much smaller. Like other monkeys who communicate using color, mandrills have very sharp eyesight for picking out colors in the gloom.

MANDRILL

Where do they live?
In small patches of rainforest and mountain forest in western Africa. They are seriously threatened by loss of habitat.

Length (male): up to 28 inches
Weight (male): up to 55 pounds

Bearing young
Females give birth to one baby at a time, usually at night, in the tree where they sleep. The bond between mother and baby is strong and lasts for many years.

Mandrill

With their vivid red and electric-blue faces, sharp teeth, long dark coats, and stumpy tails, male mandrills are among the most striking of all monkeys. The male mandrill's brilliantly colored face and rear end are used for communication. They warn other males to keep away from his territory. The bright colors also help members of his family to identify him in the dark shadows of the forest floor, where mandrills spend much of their time searching for food. At night, they climb into trees to sleep. Mandrills usually live in small family "troops" led by a huge adult male. Sometimes different troops join together to hunt for food over a wider area. They can walk long distances on their strong arms and legs.

▶ If a male mandrill draws back his mouth and lips, revealing his sharp canine teeth, and shakes his head, don't be alarmed. This is actually a friendly gesture of greeting!

▼ Despite the size and fierce appearance of the males, mandrills are sometimes attacked by large eagles as they forage on the forest floor for fallen fruit, nuts, and insects. Working in pairs, one crowned hawk eagle distracts the male while the other pounces on a young, defenseless mandrill which has become separated from the rest of the family troop.

OTHER AMAZING MONKEYS

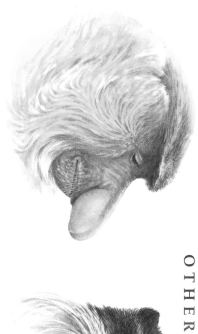

Proboscis monkey
The male proboscis monkey uses his extraordinary trunklike nose as a kind of trumpet. He warns enemies away with a loud honking or snorting noise. His large nose also attracts females during the mating season.

Emperor tamarin
The emperor tamarin's dramatic, curling mustache helps other members of its species to identify it among the forest trees.

Uakari
The bizarre-looking uakari has a bald head and a bare red face. Its face becomes even brighter in color when the monkey is excited or angry. The color fades, however, if the uakari stays out of the sun for any length of time.

Fantastic fish

What do you think of as a typical fish? A beady-eyed creature with a round body, triangular tail, and triangular fins? Many fish do look like this. But many are designed differently, with special features to help them move around, find food, defend themselves, and hide from their enemies.

▶ The weird-looking mudskipper spends much of its life out of the water. It uses its front fins as legs to crawl or "skip" along the ground.

▲ A third of a swordfish's body is taken up by its long, pointed snout, which is shaped like a sword. Swordfish are fast swimmers. The sword helps make them even more streamlined as they speed through the ocean. It is also used as a lethal weapon to slash through schools of fish.

▼ Garden eels live in groups on the seabed. Their tails are buried in the sand, leaving their heads and bodies to wave around. They come out of their burrows at sunrise to feed on tiny creatures in the water. If threatened, they vanish again.

▲ The electric eel kills its food with a short, sharp shock. Special muscles work like tiny batteries all along its body and tail. These can produce enough electricity to stun a person, although the eel preys on small fish.

▲ The porcupine puffer fish gets its name from the long, sharp spines that cover its body. When it is frightened, it gulps itself up to twice its normal size. This makes its spines stick out, so that it looks more like a pincushion than a fish.

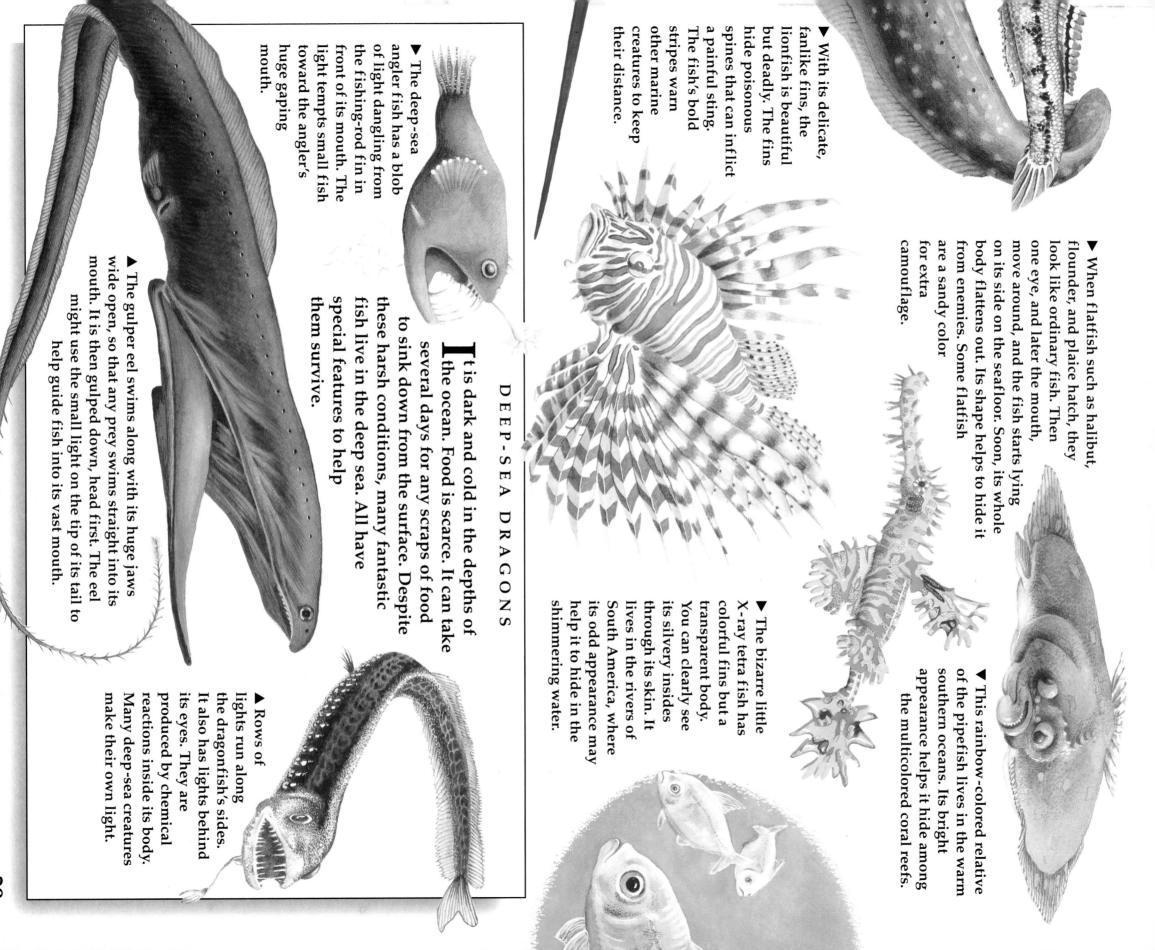

▶ When flatfish such as halibut, flounder, and plaice hatch, they look like ordinary fish. Then one eye, and later the mouth, move around, and the fish starts lying on its side on the seafloor. Soon, its whole body flattens out. Its shape helps to hide it from enemies. Some flatfish are a sandy color for extra camouflage.

▶ With its delicate, fanlike fins, the lionfish is beautiful but deadly. The fins hide poisonous spines that can inflict a painful sting. The fish's bold stripes warn other marine creatures to keep their distance.

▶ The bizarre little X-ray tetra fish has colorful fins but a transparent body. You can clearly see its silvery insides through its skin. It lives in the rivers of South America, where its odd appearance may help it to hide in the shimmering water.

▶ This rainbow-colored relative of the pipefish lives in the warm southern oceans. Its bright appearance helps it hide among the multicolored coral reefs.

DEEP-SEA DRAGONS

It is dark and cold in the depths of the ocean. Food is scarce. It can take several days for any scraps of food to sink down from the surface. Despite these harsh conditions, many fantastic fish live in the deep sea. All have special features to help them survive.

▶ The deep-sea angler fish has a blob of light dangling from the fishing-rod fin in front of its mouth. The light tempts small fish toward the angler's huge gaping mouth.

▶ The gulper eel swims along with its huge jaws wide open, so that any prey swims straight into its mouth. It is then gulped down, head first. The eel might use the small light on the tip of its tail to help guide fish into its vast mouth.

▶ Rows of lights run along the dragonfish's sides. It also has lights behind its eyes. They are produced by chemical reactions inside its body. Many deep-sea creatures make their own light.

Glossary

Alga (plural: algae)
A very simple type of plant. Some algae are only the size of a single cell. Others are much larger. Seaweed, for example, is an alga. They have no true stems, roots, or leaves, and do not produce flowers. Most types of algae live in water, but they also grow in damp soil and on tree trunks.

Camouflage
A way of blending in with the background to avoid being seen. Many animals use colors, strange shapes, and special patterns to help make themselves difficult to see.

Carrion
A dead animal, or rotting meat, eaten by an animal that has not killed it.

Crustacean (plural: crustacea)
An animal with a hard shell and usually many jointed limbs, such as crabs, lobsters, and shrimp. Most live in water.

Echolocation
A way of finding objects by using sound. Animals, such as bats, give out short bursts of high-pitched sound. These bounce off objects and the echoes are picked up by the bat. The echoes tell the bat where and how far away the object is.

Fungus (plural: fungi)
Mushrooms, toadstools, and molds are all fungi. They have no leaves, flowers, or roots, and do not make their own food as green plants do. Instead, they get their food from dead plants and animals.

Habitat
A particular type of place where an animal or plant lives. Some examples of different habitats include rainforests, deserts, grasslands, wetlands, and coral reefs.

Invertebrate
An animal without a backbone, such as a worm, spider, or insect. Animals with backbones, such as fish, reptiles, birds, and mammals, are called vertebrates.

Larva (plural: larvae)
The young of many animals. Larvae may look completely different from the adult. For example, a grub is the larva of a beetle, a tadpole is the larva of a frog, and a caterpillar is the larva of a butterfly.

Mammal
An air-breathing animal with a backbone that has hair and feeds its young on milk. For example, zebras, whales, monkeys, sea lions, and porcupines are all mammals.

Monotreme
A mammal that lays eggs, unlike most mammals, which give birth to live young. There are only two types of monotremes — duck-billed platypuses and echidnas.

Nocturnal
Animals that are active at night, rather than during the day, are called nocturnal.

Pollination
The way pollen is transferred from the stamens (the male parts of a flower) to the stigmas (the female parts of a flower). When a flower has been pollinated, it starts to make seeds. Flowers may be self-pollinated, or they can spread their pollen on the wind or by insects such as bees and butterflies.

Predator
An animal that hunts and kills other animals for food.

Prey
Animals that are hunted and killed by other animals for food.

Savanna
Large expanses of tropical grassland with a few scattered trees and bushes.

Venom
A poison made by an animal.

Index